to be love's advocate...

Say I To You

Copyright © 2020 Yon Starling

All rights reserved. No part of this book may be reproduced in any form or by any electronic or mechanical means, including information storage and retrieval systems, without permission in writing from the publisher, except by reviewers, who may quote brief passages in a review.

ISBN 978-1-7354822-0-0

Cover design by Agata Rodriguez
Interior layout design by Agata Rodriguez

Printed in the United States of America

Say I To You

Love poems by Yon Starling

Contents

I	1
II	3
III	4
IV	5
V	6
VI	7
VII	8
VIII	9
IX	10
X	12
XI	15
XII	16
XIII	17
XIV	18
XV	19
XVI	20
XVII	21
XVIII	22
XIX	23
XX	24
XXI	25
XXII	26
XXIII	27
XXIV	29
XXV	30

Yon Starling

I

Should love find me
may it perch in my heart
like the sparrow flits
from branch to branch,
a tiny song resplendent with chatter
and the joy of reuniting,
a flutter cascading in the
tremors of every leaf,
like the quiver in anticipation
of a long promised touch.
Should love find me
may it wet my eyes
like the rivulet of dew
condensed on the shiny cheek of grass,
arched by the confines of pleasure
and the bearable, yet unbearable weight,
cast in the warm palette of the morn
encapsulating the bright visage of the sun
turning molten gold
as if touched by mystical alchemy.
Should love find me
may it alight on my lips
as the bee shakes the flower
with an inelegant kiss
deep in the velvet recess
of a burgeoning bud,
jewel like in the interior
the signet of authority
impressed upon the tongue
afraid to taste but for the sting.
Should love find me
may it be worn

Say I To You

as a watery cloak
shimmering as the mist
clings to my desiccated form,
the persistent scratch of wool
a burn with every blow
seeping into my hollows,
skin pallid and cracked,
desperate to lap again at the spring,
should love find me.

II

To write of beautiful love
is to write your name
as a shooting star writes in light
across the universal sky
shedding its fragments
to grant the spellbound wish.
It is the portrait
in the pot of spilled ink
from which I spell my confession
with the clinging flourish of calligraphy.
It is to sequester my words
behind the wrought iron
curvature of my lips
until building in resonance
our song emerges
leaving me silent again.

III

Strip my flesh until my bones are chimes in the wind
that I may grate against the crooked branch
til dismembered by my own dismay.
Pluck out my eyes that I shall never see you again
in my hollow stares peering
into the forever depths of black.
Excise my tongue that once held yours
but tastes now only sorrow and blood
writhing in the salt of your phantom kiss.
Scourge my fingertips until the marrow shows
through the blank ridges split
nameless but when you called me.
And with that name seal me up in fate
and command me to despair
if our love no longer be.

IV

It is upon thine eyes,
those slow steady pools,
depth of the sky,
blanket of the deep,
stillness of the dark,
I entreat in silence.
If lover I am,
my hand ever caressing,
tender as satin,
roving in meditation,
unsteady as the fawn,
only when your gaze beckons.
If poet to be,
breaths doled out in meter,
punctuated whispers,
lyrics gently yielding,
each rhyme persuading,
should thine ears anoint me.
If sinner I am cast,
my torment everlasting,
dagger-like desire,
flesh forever yearning,
pain of my confession,
it's of the mold you made me.
For I am not, but what you see.

V

My hand, it holds yours still,
the gentle, loving hand
as if bathed in milk.
My fingers still recall
their positions betwixt yours,
each solemnly awaiting it's missing pair.
Once clasped, I still remember
our smiles matched and eyes alight
upon meeting in basic touch.
Your grip, even still now calms me,
muted promise though it is
to be in your grasp again

VI

It is not your love for which I pray.
It is not that you'll be mine.
In my most earnest wishes,
it is not your hand I seek.
Of fortune, I do not ask,
to lead your heart to me.
My prayer is said sincerely,
that love upon you shine.
Though my wish were granted,
my hand it may not be.
Should it remain to chance,
your heart shall not mislead.
If in your chest my prayer settles,
our love, sanctioned by the divine.
If in your hands, my wish you cup
I'll pour more out to thee.
If fate then has acquiesced
forever our hearts shall cleave.

VII

Your kiss is in the wine I suck.
Red as your nimble lips.
I grow heady with each eager sip,
but refuse a proffered second cup.
Another round is slight temptation,
meager substitute it is,
promise of merely shallow bliss.
Your mouth the best intoxication.
This glass hints at your sweet perfume,
a bouquet more potent than a rose.
However strong, it's only close,
your scent the greater bloom.
I draw thee in with every breath,
fresher than the early spring.
Let me share the air you breathe,
to feel you heave within my chest.
In this nectar, tastes your sweet bite,
every drop your kiss condensed.
Agony of our present tense,
when soon our rapture no more delights.
One last draft my cup upends,
its parting glance sears my heart.
The wincing pain as our lips part,
and so we seek love's amends.

VIII

Recoil not when you see me,
the rope-like scars I bear,
gauze-like purple skin
mottled by my veins
and all the dying colors.
Withdraw not from my grim looks,
the tear-prone eyes,
the callous of my cracked hands,
rough like timber,
and the sorrow of fallen stumps.
Fear not my bitter words,
for rest entreating,
eloquent as a scream,
the howl of my pain
empty like a sigh.
Close upon my withered form,
that I may perceive anew,
taut seams turned to cream,
bright flush upon my skin
the vigor of my stagnant blood.
Lean upon my sallow cheek,
now ran with noble tears,
smooth upon wary palms,
coarse hands in soft expression,
broken lines cleansed of foul debris.
Rejoice upon our sweet exchange,
relief on our touching,
words rich in quiet esteem,
to see beauty as you perceive
in my fullness of devotion.

IX

In my prayers I seek,
my heart it doubts,
but so moved to beseech,
to be as the tree that bears good fruit,
that she might be nourished.
For it is my faith,
with your seal upon my heart,
the flash of fire will burn within
that no torrents will quench.
My wisest hope,
that my deeds shall be good
and sins duly covered.
Honor above all
without envy or pride,
her name becomes my calling.
Before mountains and prophesy
ordain my service to her,
completed in mysterious love.
I have glimpsed how the eagle glides,
circles upon the rising heat.
How the snake slithers,
with the bending of its form.
The wind has filled my sails
and I have charged against the tides.
As the eagle soars,
let us rise above worldly concern.
As the snake coils,
let us yield to each others' will.
As we run before the wind,

Yon Starling

may we outlast the tempest,
steady in our wake.
Of love, I know not, except of her
and that this is love,
if I may learn the way to love her.
Bless these hands
and the arms that gather her
in firmness and regard,
our warmth willingly shared.
So wrapped in each other
my flesh shall be her shield
until we are one unto another
and our prayers unhindered.

X

Our love is like the darling bud,
first among the blanket of snow,
vibrant in colors pink and green,
its secrets tightly held
as we are in our intimacy.
Coaxed only to reveal
our sensitive layers,
undressing as they are,
by the bask and glow
of the increasing sun.
Let it grow in abundance
until overflowing the branches,
an invitation to touch and smell
in its splay and sticky sap.
May it be cacophonous
as the flock of birds
in those branches
tending the newborn nests.
Calls of fledgling vigor
full of hungry reaching,
echos of proud begging.
Down the aisle of summer,
trimmed in the pomp
of dandelion and clover,
singing the hymn
of the wind in the willow,
a proclamation loud as
the serenade of the cicada,
made in devotion

Yon Starling

as the trumpet of the swan,
framed in the golden light
of the long and radiant
day of the solstice.
Mirage like we stand
nude in confrontation
roiling in turbulent heat
brought only to tranquility
as attraction of lightening
between earth and sky,
drumbeat of thunder,
rolling like a steady moan,
the sere plains restored
quenched by sudden release.
And so the fruit burgeons
sweet in its delight,
skin polished against the waning noon
as the green stalks climb higher.
Wading in the fields,
tall grass rustling like a murmur,
parting at the presence
of the king and queen.
We claim our harvest
with abundance in our arms,
juice upon our lips,
meeting eye to eye
in our secret place
where the world fades
and knows no other,
to lay exhausted in the shade
of the season's long shadow.
Chilled by the twilight,
our breath emerges like smoke,
floating over the sparse lines
of defrocked branches
crisp against the blankness
of monochrome earth.

Say I To You

Billows that grow
from voided mouths
as words without meaning.
The heavy pull of inevitable sleep
silencing our star filled gazes
in which we speak our love
humming the mournful call
of the lone whippoorwill
until side by side,
we dream again,
in the cold dark night.

XI

Envy does not shade me
when I glance upon more handsome forms.
Regarding my reflection,
I smile instead of rage,
for it is no misfortune.
Though others may grimace
and cast aspersions
on my wicked face,
I do not glower.
I stumble forth
with proud bearing
of my hunched form,
battered though it is.
I shine with contentment,
a beauty and glow
more than one's gaze can encompass.
Invisible is the mark
of your touch upon me,
ceaseless in its caress,
cherished by broken skin.
Nothing can be deformed,
which so attracts your hand,
as I cannot despise,
a body that brings you close.
Should my ugliness cease
at your gilded rub,
I'll bare every wound for thee.

XII

Let me hear your voice in the morning
in chorus with the birds as they sing.
May it be a song in celebration,
approval of the union between you and me.
Let me wake in the hold of your body,
blessed by the sun which elegantly creeps.
A light that falls on us without boundary,
reluctant to rise and stir us from our sleep.
Let me find your eyes gazing softly,
and see in that stare everything I adore.
Delight in the day's unfolding promise,
to be spent together in love once more.

XIII

My heart it begs for you,
between the seconds of every day.
With every recitation of my voice,
repeating as my heartbeat,
in the silence I seek
the recesses unknown to me
where your footprints echo still.
Down the long passage,
where my heart lies awakened,
I chase you through every archway,
my voice a desperate imitation
in pursuit of our own harmony,
grateful for the lasting song,
of your reverberating calls,
however afar, guiding me still,
towards the center of myself,
where I'm with you again.

XIV

My window may be open
to the calming breeze of a fresh day.
I may look out at the silhouette of trees
against the rising sun of spring,
but it is not the morrow I consider.
Nor any day forthcoming,
for none seem as bright,
or without you, as promising.
My thoughts and my gaze
are fixed well beyond the horizon,
dwelling on distant yesteryear,
the images of us together,
my only faultless memories.
As if each could be a lifetime,
I close my eyes against the world,
shun the temptation of the present
and the reward of the future,
basking in constant recollection,
a desperate need to retain sincere fidelity.
As the branches sway
and return to silhouette,
as the shade darkens my windows
and I seek one last word
before the fall of night,
whether this day or the next,
none shall have worth
if I could never summon you.

Yon Starling

XV

Stroll among an alpine field and pluck every flower
that the petals may be kept ripe for pressing,
a stain of indigo, crimson, and marigold
diffusing in suggestive clouds of distillate
and in that tincture would be a drop of my love.
Scurry through the secret passages of earth,
chipping at the plain rock shielding rare gems,
crushing the amethyst and diamond into fine sand
poured into scintillating mandalas of spectral colors
to find a glint of my love among the shifting grains.
Step between the parched branches of the summer forest
gathering crisp tinder fragrant with oily sap,
felling every tree onto a fuel soaked pyre,
combustion coming at the merest touch of spark,
from that conflagration just an ember of my love would rise.
A love rich with fragrance, superfluous and uncontrolled
overflowing our bodies as fog settles in the valley,
a rich emollient soothing our clinging skin.
A love hard and as enduring as every crystal,
just as hidden and just as bravely sought,
coveted as the prince seeks a golden crown.
A love fiery as the stars cold and distant,
awe inspiring in their mysterious might,
a burning heat begging me to yield and cry,
I do, I do, I do.

XVI

Say to me "I am your love"
I will ask "where shall I swear my oath?"
Upon the great rocks which stand as a wall against the ocean tide,
stubborn in their strength against the repeating blows?
The moon hovering in silence over all our dreams,
its pocked face forever entrained upon the globe?
The sun, its proud accompaniment, shining steadily bright,
greeting all freely with its happy proud glow?
From the highest peak shall I shout to the cosmos,
past the end of time where light no longer shows?
Could the black cave preserve my vow in its harsh maw,
locked in the vault-like interior forever bound in echo?
Would it be magnified if whispered upon your gold pendant,
to rest in the space above your breast and all my kisses bestow?
I could bind it upon your hand, dainty and pale as silk,
to be tangled as filigree between your fingers closed?
At the altar as wishful prayer to any god that heeds,
profound in my request that my heart be unopposed?
Say to me one or all and these words I shall repeat,
"Swear I to be your blessed love until my last repose."

XVII

Can you still feel the brush of my thumb,
timid as it is, in perpetual motion,
against the empty grasp of my lonely hand,
the secret touch of its back and forth caress
waving like a palm frond in the wind,
silently pleading for a glimpse of your gentle smile
to flash white as a ray of sun through the trees
that I might follow to the peaceful clearing
and look to the sky as your beautiful face.
I count each touch as a notch on the prayer beads,
a heartfelt wish upon the tip of each digit
pressed as the sweet kiss I desire against your cheek
with idle hope that I might enter your thoughts,
a sense of the ghostly movement of my touch,
ready to compel your hand towards your lips,
to act as my surrogate and maintain our secret.

XVIII

To walk by your side is to walk through the shady glen
muffled in majestic silence where the proud oaks rise,
serene as the clear brook singing like rattled chimes.
It is to stare into the wide-eyed gaze of the ever alert doe,
tawny and soft, an inquiring stare damp with trust,
large as saucers and black and shiny as onyx,
fear and understanding expressed in the truest gaze,
encompassing the depth of our own sad yearning.
It is to dance the fertile waltz of the March hare,
steps as sudden and startling as a broken twig,
the nervous shifting energy of coveted love,
just as hidden in the showy veiled undergrowth
ever so present and quiet, secretly underfoot,
calmed by the simple delight of flowers and sun.
It is love that rises in the air as the peaceful dove,
sheltered from all harm in the bright dappled canopy,
wings beating like a flutter of hearts fleeting and pure,
coos that float among the trees as a sprightly song,
the sound of love's affirmation, forever seeking its pair.

Yon Starling

XIX

My mouth agape, I murmur nothing,
staring into a future replete with silence,
lips pursed in desperate anticipation,
paused mid embrace as if kissing your ghost,
the thirst of those finding only brackish water
when sought the sweetness of fresh springs,
to be quenched solely by inspired words,
which if persuades, must be called divine.
Words which stand as mirage like as you,
in my feverish chase, my purpose and my pursuit,
colors shimmering like flowers on the wind,
brushstrokes painted onto my tired eyes,
an undying image even in dreamless sleep,
a thought of you which will never cease
that when I startle awake with a shout
of passion once too timid to describe
as to love you is to write this poem,
even as I sit allayed in perpetual praise,
desperate as the wandering searchlight
seeks to capture in its bright, brief vision,
every word which leaves me hence fulfilled,
when with one gaze, and one poem, you are illuminated.

XX

It is for you I made my conversion
and nightly sing the songs of praise
raising my voice in sweet adoration
a joyful noise that you might be saved.
To love you is to believe every mystery,
delight in being bound to you by fate,
to bear with you, all of your sorrows
and plea you're led to glorious days.
Your name is the first I utter in prayer,
and whatever commanded, I shall obey
to be as your lamb, your sacrifice,
that I know pain if you know grace.
Alone but for my thoughts of you
within the dark of my hidden place
we are joined in secret unity
connected by love though far away.
In the night I will continue to toil,
on your behalf, I'll state our case,
and beg that my devotion serves,
so the sun now shines upon your face.
Without you then, let this be my purpose,
that my love grow and its merits hold sway,
to exchange my blessings if you be happy,
content in this until my tears abate.

XXI

With love for you I am forever sick
beyond the reach of mortal care
No balm to sooth my anguished heart
girdled by crooked, cruel hands
an icy grasp that squeezes and shakes
so my heart beats in erratic time
only finding its rhythm in unison with you.
No tonic can calm my churning stomach
boiling as the neglected pot seethes
a rising pressure that steams and scalds
laying me prone and doubled with aches
to utter your name my sole strength to stir.
No salve can cool my skin that burns
red with the cruelty of ceaseless night
radiant with passion's unexpressed flame
the bite of fire hidden in gentle inviting light
nostalgic for the breath of your exalted sighs.
No gauze can shield my tender cut
the quick that smarts in stinging air
a bleed that flows too wet to staunch
and now still seeps, immune to time
the loss allayed by your calm hand.
If denied, then I must perish
no cure but you, or death.

XXII

If you read this, without its address,
limited as we are by time and chance,
but I write it's for my special one,
would you know this poem's for you,
to celebrate your beauty and heart
if ever they could be encompassed
by such meager words as mine.
Do my eyes which gape with wonder
have the depth and thought to perceive
the sight to capture a blinding picture
what's lost beyond the realm of normal
all the lustrous details that astonish
how grateful to me they are revealed
spellbound as I am with perfect glee.
Let me speak all my words of rapture
so you may hear before this vision fades,
and tempted be to grant me pardon
when each expression a syllable in vain,
an urgent wish your departure hindered,
that this fantasy will be prolonged,
even as I love you now and always,
when it's my heart that must remain forlorn.

Yon Starling

XXIII

The promise made is our lives be joined,
to give my heart proudly to your service,
toiling to realize all the comforts of home,
to be deliberate in every detail of love,
each chore worthy to spark your joy.
A cup of tea steaming in its dish,
is but my rouse to charm your downy lips
and soften the tip of your supple tongue
that your words be sweet and never lash.
The pour of each cup a shapely arc,
a path chosen to sound a constant note
played as the painter's brushes stroke
vivid as the way the porcelain chatters,
and so begins a gleaming new day,
a sip and a sigh which are my just reward.
When remains your warm and empty cup,
sad as my hand drooping without your touch,
dry as the thirsty flower hangs its head,
sitting lonely now as the first fallen petal.
To clear the setting is to gather you up,
balanced in firm and steady hands,
precariously kept that we may repeat,
a ritual dependent on all made clean.
The scrub of the brush my pure delight
until polished as white as your glossy teeth
to be set in the cupboard prim and neat
right as the curtsy of girlish nobility.
As devoted to you I am my tasks,
without pause the room's decorum reset,

Say I To You

to fold and place the napkins splayed,
to polish the silver that adorns our plates,
the chairs pushed under and squarely aligned,
the table washed of all remnant crumbs.
When straight stands all as a soldier,
my duty to check the gloves report,
the light shone on the sturdy floor.
Whether chase away footprint or mote,
the drag of the broom in its rhythmic pace,
yellow straw bowed before your gilded feet.
With the pail filled and the mop to soak,
the gathering of suds in its braided cords,
dirt entangled in the draw of every stroke,
leaving naught but the bright sheen of its pull,
that your steps met with fragrance and reflection.
When all is neat, if devoted in my habits,
your first sight upon returning be a daily gift,
a room that lights as brightly as your smile,
envelops you, as I, like a heavy coat.
Once shed the blows of the finished day,
in simplicity we find a return to grace,
as quotidian tasks over all imbue,
shades of trust and meaning profound.
Though not all perfect and some undone,
in this expression there is no simple life,
dressing our home is to defy entropy,
as our love endures and restores all order.

XXIV

She is the warrior I fear the most.
Her strikes cannot be parried,
the wounds inflicted shall never heal.
Her eyes inspire fear and longing,
that I cower before her terrible stare.
My shield raised and sword in hand,
defiantly I pose, yet still I tremble,
secure within the plates of my armor,
while she, ever calm, stands proudly bare.
Against my siege she looms unassailed,
her mysterious face defiant and cold.
With scarcely a movement I am evaded,
blind to her every piercing thrust,
the barb which meets my heart and rends,
until staggered I clench my fist in dust.
Mercy I cry and beg her blows to cease,
landing unopposed with renewed ferocity.
At her most subtle movement I wince,
a pain which no distance can repel,
a chest that stings as if covered in welts,
shallow breaths drawn with an airless hiss.
Locked in the shell of my steely skin,
aches cannot break my heart's resolve,
valves which flutter and pump again,
scalded by the raging of my iron blood.
To love her is to live in awe and terror,
for mercy cry and beg her blows to cease,
no choice given but continue in defeat,
when by her single word, I am slain.

XXV

In the end, let me rest upon your name
that in repetition becomes my stern rebuke
and bites my cheeks with astonished breath.
Let love be evident in my ceaseless questions,
with hope among my many invitations to please
that I love enough to overcome all doubt.
My eyes when filled with you will shine,
a pearly light larger than the somber moon,
bathing us alone beyond that gossamer veil.
Our hands clenched with need for one another
in a grip as firm as if carved from stone
that we follow the trail beyond our darkest sleep.
Chest against chest and entangled in our arms,
held in nakedness stronger than any gravity,
we shall drift as the light shines upon the sea.
My fingers will be as the water through your hair,
currents parting the strands into flowing rows,
as I float upon your touch weightless as the stars.
The vastness of the sea condensed to a small pool,
black with stillness as a keyhole to the heavens,
calmed by the cadence of our synchronized breath.
My love shall be a litany as steady as the waves,
professed with the fervor of the siren's song,
united by harmony that we shall always be one.
From the opulence of our bed we will be reborn,
until the time we slip past the curtain of night
and our bodies become the gate that frames the sun.

Lightning Source UK Ltd.
Milton Keynes UK
UKHW011010210820
368606UK00001B/192